VIR-TAN-ZA (vûr-TAHN-zə) n. [neologism]

1. A condition, state, or attitude of truth, financial success, and customer loyalty among business-to-business sales professionals. 2. Courage in the face of adverse business cycles or uncommon challenges. 3. Commitment to the highest degree of preparedness in business dealings resulting in outstanding professional and personal achievement. 4. A process for creating exceptional solutions to sales challenges, exceeding a customer's expectations. [From Latin *vir*, "strength, heroic courage," *veritas*, "truth," and *bonus*, "a great good, a superior benefit, a bonanza."]

"Over 300 proposals were sold after using the HDS Virtanza sales training and certification program. Our sales teams are now better trained to discuss ROI advertising and marketing programs. This education program has helped us grow sales in local digital and print revenue from existing and new customers."

Dix Communications

"The HDS Virtanza training program has helped Detroit achieve strong digital revenue growth. We are big fans of the sales training and anticipate that it will continue to help us build revenue."

Detroit Media Partnership

"The Sales Training and Certification Program helped our local sales team increase digital revenue thirty-four percent year over year. We now have a very large percentage of our sellers who are certified and aggressively helping our customers to reach their customers through digital advertising."

Portland Oregonian

Virtanza

The Art and Science of Successful Selling for the
Business-to-Business Sales Professional

Debbie Holzkamp

authorHOUSE®

AuthorHouse™
1663 Liberty Drive
Bloomington, IN 47403
www.authorhouse.com
Phone: 1-800-839-8640

Published by AuthorHouse   10/19/12

ISBN: 978-1-4772-7200-8 (sc)
ISBN: 978-1-4772-7199-5 (dj)
ISBN: 978-1-4772-7198-8 (e)

Library of Congress Control Number: 2012917969

Contents

To Steve, Charlie, and Ryan
For all their sacrifices, support, and love

Robert "Pal" Wilson, ca. 1927

Introduction
The Story Behind the Creation of Virtanza: Committing to a Vision

It all starts with family, always. In the careers of my influential grandfathers, Robert "Pal" Wilson, whose work with the *Chicago Tribune* would span more than forty years, and Clarence "Chic" Holzkamp, consummate sales professional, are the inspirational and educational forces in my professional life. We all try to do our best for our families, and, if we're lucky, that usually means that we learn and grow from them in the process, and are supported in turn by them as we pursue our dreams.

My own family too often had to let go of their own dreams to follow me in my career and vision. Most of those career changes involved professional roles that were extremely high-pressure, major-responsibility, extreme situations where companies needed aggressive sales turnarounds. My quest to help companies and their sales teams to grow their sales meant that my family moved four times over the past twenty-five years, from South Florida to Des Moines, Iowa, then to Philadelphia and finally to California, our home now for ten years.

While I enjoyed sales executive leadership roles and gave over a hundred hours a week to leading and helping sales teams build customer solutions that would have results for all involved, I found over time that I had a burning desire to provide coaching and training to sales professionals full-time. One day I said to my husband, Steve, and my sons, Charlie and Ryan, "I want to quit my executive role—the one that has provided a large part of our living—to start a professional consulting and sales training company." As I said this to them, I felt an inner confidence growing that this was the right path for me to take. Of course, we had very little investment money to start this business. But, I had a strong desire that had been growing for years. While Steve, Charlie, and Ryan had some understandable concerns about this entrepreneurial venture, they gave me the support, patience, and love to begin and continue along this path. In doing so, they, too, realized they could pursue their own dreams. This decision has led all of us toward realizing our individual gifts, and toward understanding that we can cultivate and share those gifts in ways that are both satisfying and rewarding.

Although the brand of Virtanza is new, I had been developing the concept for many years. I began thinking early on about how the power of digital news media could be harnessed and what needs it would not meet, could never meet, but could only serve. And, although Virtanza makes full use of the complete array of communications tools available to us in the twenty-first century, I knew that my approach would center not only on the application of technology and those seemingly limitless wonders, but on the personal relationships that are the absolute foundation of any successful selling.

The road to this realization was far from smooth, however. The creation of Virtanza actually started when I was in my previous executive roles, managing large, 450-person sales teams. Although we achieved results, I always felt that I never had time to focus on training the staff to accomplish more. My sense of something being amiss with this scenario only grew over the years, until I finally had to admit to myself that when we are forced to do too many things, we don't do any of them well enough.

Most of all, I had an intense and growing frustration at being unable to help my staff as much as I wanted to and as much as they wanted me to. There was no time to go more deeply into their experiences with customers and find ways to solve recurring problems. We worked at such a rapid pace and under such intense pressure that nobody felt satisfied. Everyone believed they could do better if only they had the time to step back and evaluate their goals and methods.

The over-extension of my supervisory responsibilities that so thwarted my wish to have a greater impact is also what eventually sent me on the career trajectory that has led to Virtanza. I embarked on the change from business executive to entrepreneur and full-time training professional, knowing that there had to be a better way to serve customers than the traditional, rapid, and intensive, swoop-in-and-out approach.

During my transition from executive to entrepreneur, I was fortunate to have the opportunity to launch the *OC Post* in August 2006, a compact daily newspaper for time-starved people. The idea for this innovative newspaper came from my mentor, coach, and boss, Christian Anderson, then Freedom Communications Metro Group president and publisher of the *Orange County Register*. He taught me the content-publishing business. He has incomparable vision and could see there was a consumer need for a compact, edited, brief-format, local newspaper. He gave me the extraordinary opportunity to be part of its development and to lead its launch as publisher. It was quickly a success with time-starved people—we boasted more than 28,000 subscriptions within a year.

This format was ahead of its time and would have suited the iPad perfectly today—a mere six or seven years later. There were twenty different subject editors, and the *OC Post's* content ran from local news and ads to international news, from business reporting to entertainment and sports—all presented in the compact form of a daily briefing. Although I left this terrific project to start Virtanza, its meteoric rise was testament to the vision and management that made it happen; however, it too fell victim to the 2007 economic collapse and closed after a year and a half, lacking the financial support of its founders or sufficient advertising revenues in the midst of the deep recession.

However—and this is key to the Virtanza philosophy— out of these adverse trends and business cycles, a tremendous opportunity arose for me to begin to realize my vision of a more focused sales training process that would lead to more successful, long-term, business-to-business sales.

The opportunity began with a consulting job in August 2007 at Nielsen, on their business media side. My colleague at the *Miami Herald*, mentor, and dear friend of seventeen years at that time, Sabrina Crow, was their senior vice president, and she was interested in developing a sales training program that incorporated business-to-business ads in a digital way. We started to sell bits and pieces of training appropriate to the business media teams—they had over fifty titles, six regional offices of sales teams—and we conducted sales training programs with them several times over two years.

Out of these ideal training conditions and over the next three years, I developed what would become the Virtanza process of consultative selling for business-to-business sales professionals. Within five years of starting to create this method, it was ready to be launched. In February 2012, the Virtanza brand was trademarked and the process has been successfully implemented at a variety of corporations with a growing list of clients, including Dix Communications, Detroit Media Partnership, and the *Portland Oregonian*.

Finally, as with any new creation, we needed to find the best possible name. To reflect the uniqueness of our cutting-edge approach to business-to-business sales, I knew we needed a comprehensive and arresting name. I wanted a word that would express our professional ideals, reflected in our motto: "knowledge, financial success, and loyalty." We found no single word that would fit the bill, so, in keeping with our solution-oriented approach to needs, we invented one! We created our name with Latin word roots, using the authority of the old to create the excitement of the new. By tweaking several words, including the Latin words for "courage" (*vir*) and "truth" (*veritas*) and combining them with a word that powerfully connotes financial success—"Bonanza!"—we found Virtanza! A highly effective, innovative and return on investment-proven method of growing business-to-business sales was branded, and my long-held vision was realized.

This book is the first in a series of three volumes that will not only accompany my consultative business selling practice, HDS Premier Consulting/Virtanza, but will also extend Virtanza's reach to business-to-business sales professionals at all stages of a career. The present volume, *Virtanza: The Art and Science of Successful Selling for the Business-to-Business Sales Professional,* presents the fundamentals of the distinctive Virtanza approach to business sales, including its philosophical and theoretical bases, and the four trademarked, practical steps to sales training and customer sales. The second book will focus on coaching sales people through the selling process in business-to-business professional sales. The third book will present the next level of "strategic" selling at a higher level of investment in "professional" selling, which incorporates the skills of "innovative" selling. It is my hope that all those in our profession who seek to excel, to embrace the challenges of these times, and to provide the finest in consultative business selling to their customers will find in Virtanza both the inspiration and the practical skills to achieve their goals and those of their customers.

Acknowledgments

No project on the scale of creating Virtanza or writing and publishing this book is accomplished overnight or without the help and skill of many colleagues, friends, and family members. They have been treasured mentors, go-to advisors, and the source of my joy and satisfaction in life. To them go my profound thanks and warmest acknowledgement:

First, and most of all, to Steve Shary, my husband of more than twenty years, and to my sons, Charlie Taylor and Ryan Shary, I give my deepest thanks for their patience, love, and constant support as I worked to achieve this lifetime goal.

To my mother, Margie Holzkamp, whose example of constancy, belief in all people, strong faith, and loving commitment has lighted my way throughout my life.

To my sister, Susan Holzkamp Wiberg, who has inspired me with her amazing commitment to the care of her family and of others, to the practice of her relationship to God, and to her unfailing pursuit of what it means to be a great coach.

To my father, Robert Holzkamp, for his mentoring of my career over the past twenty-eight years, and for sharing with me his brilliance in the field; and to his wife, Jane Davis Holzkamp, for her boundless energy and enthusiasm in service to others, and for her valuable comments during the early days of the formation of HDS Premier Consulting.

To Sabrina Crow, more than colleague and mentor, as close as any sister, my genius of a friend for more than twenty-three years. She brought vision, clarity, quick resolve, and a belief in my talents like no other.

To Renee Ward, the executive vice president and sales director of HDS Premier Consulting and the Virtanza Sales Training and Certification program, for adding value to our program through her extraordinary communication, design, and sales skills, which are like no other I know, and for her excellent feedback on the manuscript.

To Keith Gilpin, sales and marketing consultant and direct marketing genius, for branding and marketing Virtanza using traditional and new and emerging media, and for his help, also, in editing the manuscript of this book.

To Lelani Kroeker for helping to inspire and launch the Virtanza brand, and to Will Shaw at Taphouse Graphics for making Virtanza's name development and logo design both enjoyable and enlightening.

To Chuck Dix, chief executive officer, and Ron Waite, senior vice president, of Dix Communications for helping to create and support the Virtanza methodology.

To Kylie West, a very talented writer and editor, for her excellence and professionalism in proofreading and line-editing the manuscript.

To Sylvan Creekmore, for her excellent editorial assistance in image research and selection, computer savvy, and insightful editorial critique.

To Terry Johnson, Rory Beall, Rick VanDeventer, and the design team at AuthorHouse for their enthusiasm and patience in guiding this project to publication.

And, to Rhonda Shary, for partnering with me in the co-authorship of this book, helping me to organize, express, and publish my vision.

Part I: The Art, Science, Passion, and Pride of Business Selling

Chapter One
Recognizing Your Mentors, Coaches, and Role Models

I come from a family of visionaries.

We see the world as a place filled with compelling possibilities. We were all blessed with the desire to create opportunities for ourselves, our children, and our communities. We have an innate sense of commitment; we never quit until we've achieved what we've set out to do. I have learned at the knees of these visionaries, and by their examples.

As you can readily see from the sketch of my career in the introduction, many people have been instrumental in training me professionally and in giving me support and guidance as I sought to improve and expand my skills. We all know how indispensable such knowledgeable, inspired, and inspiring people are not only to our own career success, but to the success of all business-to-business sales in the industries in which we work.

Here, however, I want to focus on the indispensable lessons I've learned from some other coaches. Past and present, my family members have always been my mentors, coaches, role models, and inspiration. They are the human faces behind my professional career and the source of my values and my drive to succeed. I offer these stories here not only out of pride in their accomplishments and their constancy to fundamental values, but also as a possible source of inspiration for you, readers and sale professionals, and as a model for how we identify those people in our lives who become our lifelong "coaches." Although this is my family story, perhaps it is not unlike your own, too.

A Family of Sales Professionals ... and Lifelong Coaches

Clarence E. Holzkamp was called "Chic" by his friends—and that means everyone he met—and "Papa Chic" by my sister and me—his granddaughters. He was a born salesperson—a consummate sales professional, whose famed ethic of customer loyalty in all his business dealings deeply informs Virtanza's motto of "knowledge, financial success, and loyalty."

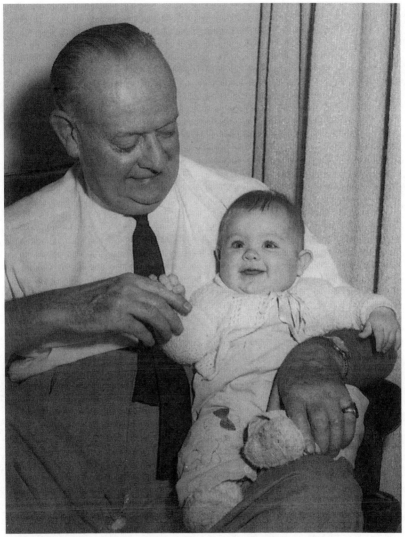

"Papa Chic" with the author, his granddaughter, ca. 1961

Papa Chic was born in 1897 in Brooklyn, and lived for much of his life in New York, although he set down roots later in the heartland, eventually passing away in Elk Grove, Illinois in 1974. His life and career are inextricably linked to American history and with one of the greatest products in American industry, perhaps *the* signature product, the automobile. Papa Chic served during both World Wars, along with his peers in The Greatest Generation. In WWI, he rode a sidecar through battlefields as an Army sergeant, suffering from shell shock for a year afterwards. When he recovered, he sought to build a career and a family, and became a Packard salesman in downtown New York City, eventually buying three Packard outlets in Westchester County. During WWII, Chic was recruited by the Army to organize all the motor vehicles at Fort Dix, New Jersey that were bound for England, France, and Germany. He was able to return to his wife and child in New York only on weekends. After the war, he met up with the legendary Earl William "Madman" Muntz, and worked for his car dealerships, including his famous, innovative Kaiser-Frazer dealership.

Deciding to pursue new opportunities in the Midwest, Chic approached General Motors in Chicago, and was offered the franchise on their Lincoln Park Buick dealership, which he bought and ran with tremendous success from 1949 until his retirement in 1958. Among his closest friends in the Chicago area was a newspaperman, Robert K. Wilson, who had begun working at the *Chicago Tribune* in 1925 in advertising sales, and would rise through the ranks to become sales manager of Financial Display Advertising.

"Pal" Wilson had a close association with top executives in the banking industry and earned a reputation as an outstanding professional with high ethics and morals. He was also well known as being reliable and well informed. He was a mathematical genius and could do instant calculations with no "adding machine," and as a result of his genuine friendliness, he was nicknamed "Pal." He retired after forty-six years with the same company. Over the years, he bought several cars from Chic, whom he took under his wing and showed around town— and, it is said, instigated the marriage of his daughter, Margie, to Chic's son, Robert, while spending afternoons test driving Chic's inventory!

Like so many Americans of this era, they not only survived, but triumphed over, the travails of the wars and the Great Depression. They were among the millions who helped build the greatest economy the world had ever known, loved their families, and set an example that would lead us into the twenty-first century while maintaining their nineteenth century values of hard work, honest dealing, and respect for people.

Robert Holzkamp atop his father's Packard inventory,
White Plains, New York, ca. 1937

Robert Holzkamp, my father and the youngest of Chic's three sons, was born in White Plains, New York, in 1932. He began his career in newspaper publishing in the classifieds department at the *Chicago Tribune* and remained with the Tribune Company throughout his forty-two-year career, again illustrating his family traits and deep professional qualities of loyalty and perseverance. During his career, Robert spent several years at the *Orlando Sentinel* and also served as general manager of the *Fort Lauderdale News and Sun-Sentinel* when the Tribune Company entered the then-burgeoning Florida market. At retirement, he was the vice president of sales and marketing for the Tribune Company, having built a national reputation for his industry-shaping skills in maximizing the opportunities of the market and the media in ways that increased advertising revenues and built stronger relationships between the advertising and news departments. He was also pioneering in the development of the talents of sales professionals, including of women, during a time when this was not often done. He recalls that, after the first women were hired in the early 1960s to sell classified ads over the telephone, they quickly rose to become over half of the entire classifieds staff. Among those whose brilliant careers he helped bring along within the Tribune family were Kathy Waltz, who became publisher of the *Orlando Sentinel*; Linda Hastings, who was sales director at the *New York Daily News* and later vice-president of advertising at the *Baltimore Sun*; Barbara Swanson, who was advertising director for the *Chicago Tribune* and has since been vice president for several other companies; and me, his grateful daughter, whose career has been enriched and wisely counseled by him.

Margie E. Wilson Holzkamp, my mother, began a career as a home sales real estate agent in 1968 while simultaneously raising a family and managing a household. She loves to sell and thinks of it as building relationships and establishing communities. She recently renewed her real estate license at age seventy-five and plans to retire after over forty years in service to her community. She believes in the inherent value of "all kinds of people," as she puts it—clearly, another inspirational source for my bedrock philosophies behind Virtanza.

Susan H. Wiberg, my sister, is a certified professional ski instructor and a high school ski racing team coach for both boys and girls. She is deeply committed to motivating, training, and coaching young people to be their best. In fact, one of her students placed first in the state of Michigan in the High School Girls Slalom in 2011–12. While working at Abbott Labs, she trained and coached people in the administration of the first AIDS tests, and later, in the use of diagnostic products in hospitals, labs, and doctors' offices.

My sons, Charlie and Ryan, who are now beginning to build their own careers, were both members of champion football teams in high school. Charlie was later hired after graduation as an assistant coach. Ryan, a true Californian, was a member of his high school's surfing team as well. While still a college student himself, Charlie was a teacher and coach for other students in the design of unmanned aircraft. And Ryan is now working in retail sales at a Laguna Beach surf shop and studying to attend law school with a vision to change the world for the better.

My husband, Steve Shary, has been a champion athlete since the age of nine, competing on the Junior Davis Cup team in tennis, winning state and regional championships with his high school basketball team, and continuing to coach young people in basketball and football to this day. His career has included selling financial services and products, investing in community home improvement, and, now, selling luxury and vintage automobiles

When I was first starting out in sales, my grandfather, "Pal" Wilson, gave me a copy, now yellowed with age, of the professional guidelines from the advertising and sales division of the *Chicago Tribune,* where he would rise to become a sales manager. They were called "The Rules of the Road" and they are a testament to the early guidance and support I received from my family members, both directly and by "osmosis."

Think back over your personal history, investigate your family story, and see whether there are patterns and people who show desires and goals similar to your own. Strive to keep up mutually supportive relationships with these people. Keep in good contact, and be prepared to listen to their life stories, struggles, and achievements. This is not only how you create a lasting, mutual friendship, but it is how you learn about others, about the world, and, perhaps most importantly, about yourself.

There are many wonderful resources for professional development available even if you find that your current circle still does not meet your needs for supportive mentoring and regardless of whether you are early, mid, or late in your career. There are excellent personal guidance books as well as high-level professional development seminars and workshops, where you can begin to expand your network and actively seek skills as well as people who can help advance your interests and become your best self. There are many ways to develop a relationship with a lifetime coach, and your process of identifying, nurturing, and trusting your mentor might take some turns along the way, but you will eventually find yourselves in each others' productive company if you are committed to the process.

Perhaps the most important—and maybe the most fruitful—aspect of a relationship with lifetime coach is that you must be prepared to hear feedback that you don't really want to hear.

It is essential that we are not only willing to hear criticism, *but that we seek it out*. Only in this way will we grow and learn to take the risks that are necessary for success. More on this essential point is discussed later in this book, but it applies here equally importantly. "Yay-sayers" will not get you past your weaknesses, nor will coat-tailers push you forward. Find someone who can be insightful, knowledgeable, and supportive, but who also can tell you what you need to hear, not only what you want to hear.

The Virtanza process relies on the process of mentoring, and the art of coaching. If these relationships are valued and nurtured in your private life, you will find their principles informing and enriching your professional life as well. It is essential to identify and value your lifetime coaches to a successful career in consultative selling, but also in creating a fulfilling life. Nobody gets there alone.

Chapter Two
Being Our Best on Behalf of the Customer

In order to build and sustain relationships over the long-term, the Virtanza methodology emphasizes that the sales professional bring his or her *best* self to every encounter. The goal is to develop the discipline of balancing all aspects of your life, and to make that discipline part of your daily professional and personal life, so that the strengths you bring to each are virtually indistinguishable. It is a conscious effort to combine traditional sales training with a total vision of business selling as an art, a science, a passion, and a point of pride.

The Balance of Mind, Body, and Spirit

Over the course of my career as a sales professional, during which I continued to train and compete nationally in figure skating and to enjoy an exhilarating hobby (some might accurately call it an obsession) on the slopes, I have come more and more to think of sales as a sport—a high-level, championship-oriented pursuit that occurs as much within the self as it does without.

I have also come to understand the absolute importance of achieving a disciplined balance in life if we are to be at our best. This is not a call to ninja training or extreme workout mania, but to a true and ultimately effortless balance of the main components of our human selves—the mind, body, and spirit.

Let me explain.

Mind

It is no accident that "knowledge" is first on the list of Virtanza's motto. The daily habits of reading, researching, and staying current with cutting-edge information must be built into the sales professional's daily discipline. The importance of mental sharpness and agility, of keen critical faculties is certainly a given in any high-stakes endeavor, but one could argue that accurate knowledge and critical thinking are even more important to cultivate in these times of rapid flow of information and the open sources of the Internet. We have to not only gain knowledge—to track trends in the client's field, innovations in digital technologies, and new approaches to sales—but also to discern between *good* information and poorly presented data or biased, unfounded analyses. The importance of having a wide range of information sources, news analysis, editorial and opinion from knowledgeable, respected, and highly well informed professionals cannot be overstated.

I am a self-confessed newspaper junky. My head is full of

information from a lifetime of curiosity and a daily practice of reading widely. Books on sales theory, practice, and process are particularly helpful, of course, and I have added over eighty such books to my personal reference library over recent years. It is essential to stay current on national and global economic trends and to always know the context of the business information and financial climate in which your clients are operating.

Some of the major publications and media outlets utilized regularly, if not daily, by successful professionals are: *The Wall Street Journal*, *USA Today*, and the *The New York Times*; periodicals with news analysis and substantive features like *The Economist* and *The New Yorker*; *Entrepreneur* to stay abreast of any new processes that people are using to apply sales theory; *Harvard Business Review* (one of my favorites), especially for new strategies. Trade and industry newsletters also play an important role, including those from BIA/Kelsey, as well as newsfeeds, listservs, and blogs—including Mashable. And finally, news outlets of local markets are key to being an informed salesperson, whether in print, online, or downloaded to the iPad, which is becoming a huge part of our profession (its obvious practical and strategic value is only enhanced by its value to our environment, as a paper-free platform for delivery of information and presentations). Finally, for my spiritual growth (as I discuss later), I also read the Bible, along with daily devotions and at least two spiritual books a week.

I read every morning after running several miles and throughout the day as time permits. I'd estimate that I spend one-third of my time reading—although another third of my time is spent interacting with people, whether in person or online or by another digital means. I am naturally curious and am always learning from people. The true art of sales is *here*, at the intersection of book knowledge and human interaction. At the end of the day, we need to remember that the art of sales and successful selling is as much about reading, research, digital platforms, and aggressive pursuit of opportunities, as it is about communicating with people. Staying current and informed is essential, but only in practice and application—in sharing that information and applying it to one's sales practice—does the information really become valuable. Inform your relationships with the people you are going to serve, keep your mind sharp, and the investment toward which you are going to lead your customers will be enormously enhanced.

Body

I believe so deeply in fitness as way of life and as a source of joy and self-renewal that when I say that engaging in regular, sustained, and focused physical activity is essential, it is almost like recommending to someone that he or she breathe. The benefits to the individual of this kind of disciplined pursuit of health extend to a person's professional life in immediate and measurable ways. When you are at peak performance within your body, you will be at peak performance in your work as well. You will feel great and it will show in the way you move and present yourself to customers, and in your capacity to sustain a rigorous and demanding schedule on their behalf.

I mean something more than meeting the expected standards

of professionalism, of care of the body and pride in appearance. I am interested in what is beneath our surface as well, of concern for good nutrition and a rigorous and regular exercise regime that prepares us, from our center or core, to meet the highest expectations of our profession. Through pursuit of a fitness regime, at the level that your health will allow, you will create and sustain a reservoir of physical energy that is essential to achieving the highest levels of success in professional sales.

I am thinking of an almost athletic mindset toward preparing for the sales profession. Athletes know the necessity of daily discipline, training to be the best possible, and being ready to perform at all times. I have experienced this in a profound way in my own life.

I trained as a solo and pairs competitive figure skater throughout childhood, placing first in regional competitions on several occasions. What I most loved to do then, however, was to perform with a non-competitive exhibition group, the Park Ridge (Illinois) Michael Kirby Skating Show. This preference perhaps explains, in part, my leaving skating from age sixteen until thirty-seven. It was, simply, not my passion during those years—other adolescent activities, other life paths, and career building were my focus then—and I couldn't do it only halfway.

One of my greatest "Virtanza" moments occurred more than a decade before I actually created the Virtanza sales training program, while I was the vice president of advertising at the *Philadelphia Inquirer* and *Daily News*. After over twenty years away from the ice rink, I reentered daily training—at the age of forty—with the goal of competing in the United States Adult Figure Skating Championships in Marvel, Massachusetts in March of 2000. I'm going to go ahead and tell you that I won the first qualifiers in my division, and placed third in the finals—a result of which I am very proud. It is the circumstances under which I entered that ice rink for those performances, not so much the outcome, that matter here—although, the outcome was absolutely Virtanza—that commitment to excellence, to a total engagement of all of my abilities and faculties, and to reaching a goal.

On that Friday afternoon, a few hours before the finals competition was to start, I received a call from senior management at the paper that we needed to convene a teleconference that afternoon of all managers and executives in advance of a press release that would go out on Monday. That press release would announce that the paper, hit hard by the collapse of the tech bubble, would be reducing staff by ten percent across the board. Every department would be affected and the staff would have to be informed that afternoon, after which I would then have to go out on the ice and give that my best, too.

I had to do both of the things I had trained to do every day to the best of my abilities in order to pursue a dream and reach a goal. I learned that day that you'd be amazed by what you can do, when you have to, if you are prepared.

The author in training for the US Adult Figure Skating competition,
Marvel, Massachusetts, March 2000

You have already read about the commitment to athletic pursuits that runs in my family, and the joy and skill that we strive to share with others through coaching and mentoring in many different sports, at many different levels. While not everyone will pursue a sport competitively, the kind of inner and outer well-being that comes from regular attention to the health of the body and the discipline of training is essential to maintaining a positive attitude and a readiness to "bring it" to yourself and your customers.

Spirit

Each person's spiritual beliefs and practices are, of course, fundamentally and inalienably individual and private—they are a matter of a personal relationship with God or with one's own understanding of the presence of the divine or the sacred in our lives. My own spiritual practice has been central to sustaining my positive outlook and my commitment to others. My Christian faith has been my main spiritual influence and has helped me to experience long-term success in business and in life. A deep and actively practiced faith has been the foundation of my life, informing my principles and my goals. My spiritual practice has led me to understand the importance of focusing on the people around me, to pay attention to how we can help each other, and to focus on what others are trying to achieve or to become. To put it simply, I have gained insight into what it means to say: It's about them; it's not about me.

My sister, Sue, gives generously of her time through her church, especially to the Asian immigrant community in Detroit, teaching and mentoring new residents through their adjustment to life in the United States and establishing themselves in jobs, schools, and communities. Her father-in-law, Reverend James W. Wiberg, was the pastor of Calvary Lutheran Church in Minocqua, Wisconsin— the church we attended while vacationing at our family cabin. He practices a faith rooted in valuing all people, placing no judgment on anyone, and bringing to life the central teaching of Christ to love God and to love our neighbors above all else (Matt. 22:36–40). Reverend Wiberg works from the basis that every person you meet or talk to is special in the eyes of God and in our human community.

My mother, Margie Holzkamp, believes deeply that all people are innately good; this foundation has led her to practice a deep faith in her dealings with people in life and in her career of forty-four years as a real estate sales agent. A former Sunday school teacher, my mother instilled knowledge of the Gospels in my sister and me and a strong moral foundation. I have come to appreciate this gift more as I mature into a deeper understanding of the need to build a strong foundation of moral behavior in life and in work. Helping people find homes in which to raise their families has been her passion as well as her profession. And although she will retire in 2012 at age seventy-seven, she leaves a legacy of faith-inspired work behind her that has inspired all who know her.

I find a great deal of inspiration and peace in the Scriptures, especially in times of turmoil and uncertainty, and specifically in the central passages of the Christian message:

> Love is patient; love is kind. It does not envy, it does not boast, it is not proud. It is not rude, it is not self-seeking, it is not easily angered, it keeps no record of wrongs. Love does not delight in evil but rejoices with the truth. It always protects, always trusts, always hopes, always perseveres (1 Corinthians 13:4–7).

> And now these three remain: faith, hope and love. But the greatest of these is love (1 Corinthians 13:13).

> God is love (1 John 4:8).

The profound wisdom of ages and the word of God within these passages inform my life and my approach to those with whom I come in contact.

I do not claim to be a perfect Christian—these are goals

I strive toward, but often fall short of. Nor do I intend to proselytize by including these quotations or describing my beliefs in this book. I mean instead to illustrate the necessity of seeking a spiritual truth beyond the self that will provide a source of strength and clarity in our complex and often too-driven twenty-first century lives.

Our family has approached our faith as a service-oriented practice, and it has consequently informed our career choices and provided us with a compass of integrity. Perhaps you draw upon another spiritual tradition in your daily life for guidance and inspiration; perhaps you "feed your soul" in another way altogether, apart from religious or spiritual practices. Perhaps an artistic or nature-based activity, like hiking or gardening, gives you the inner sustenance you need to maintain your perspective on your role in the world. Whatever the practice, we all need a basis on which to build a foundation of behaving honestly and compassionately toward each other, and that foundation should become an integral part of all our dealings in our business life as well.

Focus on People

If we always keep our eyes trained on the needs of others, we will succeed in our goal of providing the finest services in sales training.

An absolute rule for achieving this goal is: never prejudge people based on what you think you see or hear. Their clothing means nothing. Their haircuts, or lack thereof, mean nothing. Their accents, cars, jewelry, or shoes—even their politics or beliefs—mean nothing about the real people with whom you want to connect, whose needs and goals you must strive to understand. If you respond only to their exterior characteristics or their projected personality and make decisions about people's abilities or net worth on that basis, you will limit your potential to truly know potential customers. If you dismiss people based on their appearance, the shabbiest pair of shoes could be walking out the door along with your multi-million-dollar sale. The inverse is also true: The finest, softest Italian leather loafers or pumps could be disguising a real heel—a phony who will waste your time and, ultimately, your money.

Good books can have deceptively off-putting or discomforting covers, based on your own set of values or what is familiar and comfortable to you in your everyday world. My father recently gave me a perfect example of how to welcome and embrace every person you meet, despite the differences that might seem to alienate you from each other upon meeting: After decades of using a popular brand of computer, he and his wife decided to change brands and went shopping at the retail store devoted to the new brand. Even though they are of a generation widely thought to be computer-phobic, they are keen to learn new things, and so began to ask the very young, very tattooed sales clerk some initial questions about their options. My father said that they quickly came to understand that, despite this strange (to them) appearance, which might have caused others to dismiss this young sales clerk as a mere stock handler, this young man was highly intelligent and thoroughly knowledgeable about the product, and more—he was skilled in communicating his knowledge and in putting his customers at ease. "I experienced once again," said my father, "what I've practiced professionally my whole life: the absolute importance of treating all customers equally well, but also of never judging people, of always meeting each person with enthusiasm and an open mind."

My grandfather, Chic Holzkamp, also told a story about a day that would become legendary at the Packard luxury auto dealership where he worked in New York, a day when a very disheveled-looking man entered the showroom and poked around a while. He was studiously avoided by most of the sales staff who did not want to waste their time on someone who clearly, judging from his inelegant clothing and generally shabby appearance, could not afford their product. But Chic Holzkamp had a different philosophy about people. He believed that everyone deserved courtesy and a willing ear and that one ought *never* to disqualify people without first asking many questions and listening to the answers, and so, he approached that shabby man with respect and the intention of meeting his needs. He ended up making a sale to a member of what was at that time, and still is, among the wealthiest and most influential families in the United States, or indeed, the world.

The key to fostering this kind of attitude in yourself and in any sales team is to listen to what the customer is telling you about himself or herself that you didn't even know to ask about—to listen to the person behind the appearances. More on this subject will follow in step two of the Virtanza process of business-to-business selling, but for now, suffice it to say that, unless we listen and truly look, we will miss the person behind the sale.

Again, I find a valuable source of wisdom on this subject in my go-to Book, "Judge not, and ye shall not be judged: condemn not, and ye shall not be condemned; forgive, and ye shall be forgiven" (Luke 6:37).

The Courage to Persevere

Even in ordinary lives, we sometimes are called upon to find courage in the face of disappointments, even unexpected dangers. Often, when great rewards are at stake, great obstacles can occur, great challenges or resistance may arise. I speak more directly of experiencing obstacles in chapter four, but here, as an overview of the importance of perseverance in the life of a business-to-business sales professional, I am interested in making two observations based on personal experience of this phenomenon.

First I want to draw again on the experiences of my family members, Chic Holzkamp and Robert Holzkamp. As "men of affairs," as these newspapermen and leaders would have been described in another time, Chic and his son, Robert, would both come up against circumstances that would test their courage and determination to see their obligations through to their right, responsible conclusion.

Chic's closest friend, Gustav Allgauer, owned one of the most famous gathering places in Chicago in the 1950s, the eponymous Allgauer's Fireside Restaurant, frequented by sales and newspaper people. As it happened, the Senate Rackets Committee, of which then-junior Senator Robert F. Kennedy was chief counsel, was investigating the suspected control of various industries in Chicago by organized crime. Gustav Allgauer was asked to testify against the company that supplied the linens to his restaurant. He agreed, of course. He was the kind of man whose sense of right meant finding the courage to testify when called by his government to do so—even though it probably meant the loss of his business, which burned to the ground on May 13, 1958. Nevertheless, Gus and several other Chicago restaurant owners proceeded to testify during the week of July 13, 1958, and, in time, Gus opened a new restaurant.

Chic's son, Robert, my father, would find himself embroiled in another historic labor struggle during the early 1990s, when the Tribune Company sought to sell the financially troubled *New York Daily News*. Greater detail is given about this event in Part III of this book, but it suffices here to say that, when several unions went on strike, fearing loss of jobs and other forms of control and compensation out of the sale, fire again entered the struggle, and newsstands were burnt to the ground. Robert, however, had to keep doing his job in the midst of this dramatic conflict; he had to find the best way to lead his people, as director of sales, to the best possible outcome in the best interests of the company. He succeeded and credits the valuable discussions between the management and the union representatives as the reason for this success—although those who have worked in leadership positions or as members of a successful team know how much such success relies on the personal qualities of the one in charge.

My second observation has to do with the kinds of obstacles we encounter regularly that arise out of simple human nature. We have all had experience with difficult people in our professional dealings. Some actively seek to undermine our efforts. Others seem almost constitutionally inclined to bad behavior, rudeness, dishonest practices, or any number of other unprofessional antics. The successful sales professional learns to meet with confidence the rivalries, expectations, and limitations that will arise, predictably, from human nature.

And, consistent with the key fourth step of the Virtanza process—asking for critical feedback in conjunction with fulfilling the customer sale—if you have perhaps been one of those unprofessional or difficult people at times, honestly and purposefully take stock of your motives. Invest sincerely in the constant improvement of yourself as well as of your customer's interests. This form of courage is among the most demanding and, therefore, among the most personally rewarding.

To be a successful business-to-business sales professional, we must learn to communicate with all kinds of people. We must not dwell on setbacks or unfairness that may arise from difficult situations. Find ways to address problems positively, to create changes that will contribute your goals and those of your clients.

Persistence, habit, faith in oneself and one's purpose; a

balance of mind, body, and spirit; and maintaining the highest in professional standards will help you to be your best on behalf of the customer. These important traits will inform the core principles of Virtanza as you begin to practice them.

Chapter Three
The Virtanza Method

Virtanza is a four-step, multimedia-based sales training and certification program designed to enhance prospecting, territory management, customer relationships, and sales revenue among sales teams. Its long-term relationship building and mentoring approach uniquely and significantly permits flexibility in responding to rapidly changing media and sales contexts, and can be applied in a variety of industries and businesses.

Described in broad strokes, the Virtanza approach allows sales teams and clients the flexibility to use all effective sales tools, whether the contact is face-to-face or screen-to-screen. We incorporate these approaches into the fundamental practices developed over decades of experience in sales, focusing on a ROI (return-on-investment)-based training and certification program that encompasses the tried-and-true basics of a direct, hands-on approach to training. The result is a built-in process of accountability; a personal field call coach and mentor structure; and, a guided series of classroom trainings.

The author conducting a Virtanza training session, 2011

Finally, I created Virtanza, a customer-centered, transformational approach to business-to-business sales, out of a vision that by embracing all the exciting possibilities and challenges offered to us at the start of this twenty-first century, with its seemingly unlimited potential to generate new and better digital technologies and electronic media, we have unlimited new potential to reach clients and media communities. Where Facebook and Twitter were once cutting edge, who knows what opportunities for faster or more effective or more responsive media contact will emerge in the years—or months—to come? The Virtanza methodology embraces all these tools and future possibilities and can readily incorporate them all.

What sets Virtanza apart from any other approach to business-to-business sales? How is Virtanza different from—and more effective than—traditional or long-established methods? We can describe the four distinct attributes, and chief strengths, of the Virtanza process as having:

- A total approach to preparing for business-to-business selling that includes not only gathering sales information, researching and qualifying the customer, and generating creative ideas, but also on preparing the *self* to be in the best working condition at all times on behalf of the customer. ("Qualifying" is the process of researching a customer's background in order to assess the potential for a good match between the customer's values and needs and your sales solutions.)

- An emphasis on the art of *listening* incorporated into the art of selling, and on meeting all people on their own terms, resulting in a new and highly effective approach to qualifying.

- A design to actively reach the productive stage of *critical feedback*, to work purposefully with human nature within the realm of finance, so that the fundamental sources of the customer's discomfort with change can be identified, and recommended solutions can be constantly revisited.

- An intention to build and maintain *long-term relationships* from the outset, with expectations of future modifications over years of close, continued consultation.

Although the methodology for Virtanza grew out of my experience in the newspaper and media businesses, the core principles of Virtanza are completely transferrable to other settings. We are actively branching out from our initial expertise in the newspaper and digital publishing business to lead business professionals in other industries toward achieving their goals. When considering the effectiveness of our basic approach, it's easy to see how this transfer of principles would indeed be so immediate.

Step One. Qualifying the Customer
The Value and Purpose of Research

Qualifying the customer is the basis for all that follows in building your relationship with him or her. It is the time when you can best set up the framework for your approach to gaining a full and accurate initial picture of your customer. During this step, it is essential that you avoid jumping to conclusions about the customer, about his or her needs, and about the potential solutions for those needs. In "Focus on People" in chapter two, you read an anecdote about my grandfather's credo to never judge and disqualify a customer until you have asked enough questions and spent enough time to thoroughly understand his or her needs. You want to be sure you are able to sell that "Packard" to the customer, and not watch him or her walk away because you didn't sufficiently appreciate the people or person standing right in front of you.

Within this context, there are three basic tasks to help you formulate the best questions and the best information resources:

- Do Your Homework

  While the goal of any research is to gain deeper knowledge and broaden our understanding of a subject, in professional sales, we also seek to identify the opportunities for your customers that reveal themselves in the details of the customer's history, organizational culture, financial picture, and so forth. The more detail you can unearth and the fuller the picture you can create of this customer's past, the better prepared you will be to lead the customer into the future.

• Identify the Value You Bring to the Customer

Your research should lead you to a thorough, three-dimensional understanding not only of the customer's profile, but also of the ways in which you can intersect with the customer's interests and needs, and the skills you can bring to the relationship. You want to be able to articulate very clearly to your potential customers how you see your skills benefiting them.

• Maximize the Organization of Your Research

We are living in a time of rapid, unprecedented change in the business environment driven by technological and digital innovations. Make full use of them all! Learn them, by any means necessary. Stay current with the latest applications and software, platforms and outlets.

Communications have always been vital

to success in sales, and success is all about the communications revolution in this digital age. Research tools and information management tools are also changing rapidly; sometimes, it seems, on a daily basis. It should be part of your regular regime to stay current with media and technology as tools for your own research into potential and current customers. You should be fluent in the language of technology and its applications as part of the package of solutions for your customer's problems and needs.

Digital technology is also vital as an essential tool for organizing your communications and research over the long- and short-term. The two main categories that pertain to sales professionals are:

- Customer Relationship Management (CRM) Tools

   Something as simple as a computer spreadsheet or the products of one of many reputable software companies—currently, Salesforce.com or Saleslogix.com, among many others— will help you manage and organize your customer contacts, follow up, and continue research with maximum efficiency.

- Social Media and Technology

LinkedIn, Twitter, YouTube, Facebook, Foursquare, Pinterest—these are only a handful of products and applications of the moment that can be of enormous benefit to your research and communications; surely there will be many more before this book finds its way into your hands.

The "cloud environment" now allows us to keep customer communications, research data—everything!—current, and we can access our data from any type of platform (smart phone, laptop, desktop, tablets) and from almost any location. Innovation has always been at the heart of successful businesses, and is the lifeblood of entrepreneurial endeavors, and this digital universe in which we now operate is in a constant state of innovation. This is both useful and—very distracting! As much as we must make it our business to stay current in our knowledge and savvy in our technology usage, we must also guard against becoming overwhelmed by the plethora of technologies and applications out there. When it comes down to the practical matters of business, there are probably a limited number of technologies that will serve our customers at any given time and that their customers will be able to use. As in all other business considerations, we will have to stay ahead of the curve on technological advances, but also, know when to avoid potentially distracting options.

Step Two. Assessing the Needs of the Customer
The Art of Making Your Customer
Uncomfortable—Purposefully

In our trainings, we provide Virtanza students with needs-assessment tools, the specific scripts and methodologies to use with their target customers, developed out of years of experience and field-testing. There are individualized versions of needs-assessment tools, depending on the customer's business, that include customized training scripts and tools.

This book and the focused material presented in it is intended to give you general ideas about how to make customers comfortable enough to share extreme challenges. The *art* of this approach is in knowing *how* to reach individual people on their level in their world, guiding them to feel comfortable in revealing their greatest reservations—fears, really—about making changes in their business.

The art of making your customer uncomfortable—purposefully

To some people this skill of putting customers at ease even

when covering delicate subjects comes very naturally. For others, it might be more difficult. Some sales professionals might see that effort as aggressive or abrasive or invasive, too demanding of personal information, too disrespectful of boundaries.

But it's not. We're trying to be helpful, trying to get at the information that will ultimately prepare us to investigate what's most important to this business so we can create the best solution for them and help them financially.

Herein lies the art of an effective customer-needs assessment; if the customer doesn't show you the real problem, you won't be able to sell a solution. It won't be possible. It just won't happen.

If this is a difficult part of the process for you in business-to-business selling, then you will need to practice, work with your coaches, have colleagues give you feedback so you can become skilled and confident in getting this critical information from customers. If you don't master this art, you'll fail in this process.

And, please know that I still have to practice, all the time. I still have to work at how to help a customer share his or her needs, and how to translate those needs into a solution.

- Review Your Research

  This step may seem painfully obvious, but it is essential to have the key points about your customer fresh in your mind. Memorize details and prepare summaries. You will gain the customer's trust and respect by showing that you have done your homework.

- Generate Your Outline for the Needs Assessment

    Never go into a needs-assessment session without a clear and written outline of your purpose and your plan for achieving it. You might need to improvise or change some of its elements as you go, but it is vital that you have a clearly charted course as you embark on these important dialogues.

- Present Your Questions

    Based on your research, you will have questions tailored to each customer and for each sales situation. However, there is a list of basic questions that must be covered in every situation. The most productive of these basic questions will most likely be:

    Who is your customer's target customer base?

    What has been your customer's best way of engaging that base?

    What has not worked at all?

    What does your customer desire to achieve?

    How much does your customer typically invest in a solution? What would that investment be in terms of percentage of sales volume in a year? Is your customer willing to invest one percent of annual sales? Five percent of annual sales?

Once that investment is made, what ROI is expected, and over what time period? By when does your customer plan to make back the investment and profit from the investment?

How will your customer connect with his or her customers? What are the possible solutions for the customers to whom they are trying to sell?

Who are the key decision-makers and stakeholders? What criteria will the decision makers use in making their final investment decision?

What is the time frame of those decision-makers and stakeholders?

How urgent, on the typical scale of one to ten, is this investment?

How quickly can you get to "yes" with your customer? Will it take a long time?

What would success look like?

And, a very powerful question never to miss is the one that is calculated to elicit the most important information:

What is your customer *not* willing to do to achieve this success?

After each question, ask clarifying questions, so you can confirm beyond a doubt what the customer is saying and what he or she wants to achieve. Repeat the customer's words back to him or her in the form of a question, with an interpretation of the meaning that seems most likely to you. Ask your customer, "Did I understand correctly that you are saying ...?" Do so even if you think you're sure that you heard it right the first time. It is amazing how often what we *think* we heard turns out *not* to be what the speaker meant to express.

It is possible—indeed, likely—that your customers really do not know what has been holding them back from accomplishing their goals. They might think they have a clear general picture of their problems, their goals, and their solutions— but you must find the way to circumvent any preconceptions they might have, and instead, to lead them to the areas they have not yet explored, often because they have not yet realized that they want or need to.

Your customers might be reluctant to acknowledge what they fear most about their perceived failures or the painful challenges that they feel they cannot meet. This is precisely the uncomfortable ground you need to reach if you are to succeed in identifying needs-based solutions that it is your job—and your privilege—to develop and present to them.

- Listen to the Customer's Answers

  It is impossible to overstate the importance of this skill. It is crucial in preparing a responsive and detailed proposal, but it is also crucial in the fulfillment stage, step four, discussed below. Strive to hear exactly what the customer is saying and avoid inferring your own thoughts and responses.

- Evaluate the Customer's Position

  Finally, seek to understand the customer's answers in a global sense as well as in a highly detailed sense. Organize and analyze them in ways that will yield a cohesive vision of the needs to be addressed.

Step Three. Creating and Presenting the Customer Solution
The Proposal

You are now ready to compile and present all of the material you will have generated by researching, evaluating, asking, and listening. The customer will expect a clear set of solutions from you and you will be well prepared to develop them and discuss them with your customer after following the guidelines given here, along with the customized Virtanza methodology presented in our trainings.

- Summarize the Needs of the Customer

  At this crucial stage, you must now summarize the needs of the customer and express them in a way that describes the business goals and sales objectives of the customer. It may be that they are trying chiefly to improve profits, and that's okay. Develop solutions that would present the investment as a way to reduce costs. In any case, the customer's budget is a key part of any solution, as a percentage of sales.

- Identify the Key Parts of the Plan

  You then must identify the key parts of the plan that you are developing. How will each part of your plan match their needs? The five essential factors that any plan must address are:

  Sales Goals

  Target Audience

  Integration with Financial Conditions and Business Operations

  Timing of Implementation

  Expected Return on Investment

- Present All the Tactics for Meeting Their Goals

For example, if advertising campaigns are the main tactic to be developed, describe in detail the whole program, creating the schedule of advertisements and other details. Describe all the elements of your solution. Always present them in a direct and concrete form, like Microsoft Word or PowerPoint.

- Describe the Value of the Investment

  Sum it all up. State the value of this solution, this program, these details, in concrete terms.

- Ask for Their Commitment

  There are four main approaches to getting commitment. Choose your approach based on the individual customer and the nature of the plan you are presenting:

  Use direct language, as in, "I am asking you for your commitment."

  Make an assumption, as in, "We know you want X ..."

  Ask an open-ended question, such as, "What do you think?"

  Float a trial closing, like, "Do you think X will work?" or "Which of our plans do you think will work best?"

- Identify the Follow-Up Markers and Time Frames

  Together with the customer, identify the follow-up markers and time frames that you and the customer will follow to evaluate the proposed solutions, and to determine any necessary modifications as the process of implementing the plan develops.

  Especially important in this evaluative process is the question: how will you evaluate the return on investment?

  It is also important to remember that often, you don't get a "yes" right away. This is the step during which you listen *closely* to feedback—what does your customer like, what does he or she wish were different—and begin to develop, already, the alternative proposal(s). Be prepared, *anticipate*, the possible alternative scenarios and solutions.

  Brainstorm with the customer, and put all the ideas on paper with the customer or with your own team, prioritize them as most likely to be the best solutions, and then discuss them in depth.

Remember that rarely is the consultative selling process linear. Often, you will have to take an alternative path to gain the customer's commitment.

Step Four. Fulfilling the Customer Sale
The Art of Hearing Critical Feedback

Asking for critical feedback can be the toughest part of any sales relationship, but it's also where we learn the most, and where productive change and improvement happens. The willingness to accept critical feedback will make or break your ongoing sale.

Hearing feedback forces us to create modifications. It actually gives us better control of the sale and of our ongoing relationship with the customer. It puts us in a position of greater respect from customers because they see our willingness to listen in action.

> Critical feedback is essential to this process of identifying the right solutions. It leads to continuous improvement—the acknowledgement that we can always do better.

> How can we ensure that this key element of maintaining an ongoing relationship is always there?

> We must actively solicit the feedback from customers.

> We must practice the art of *listening*.

> We must commit to incorporating it into our practice.

> How do we prepare ourselves to receive this critical feedback? Think about how you train in

any activity. Think about the coach or teacher who gave you critical feedback all along the way. You want to *win* for the customer. The greatest coaches are able to keep us focused on that goal and to help us minimize the distraction of our ego's desires.

Learn to filter the feedback. From your professional experience, you might recognize that feedback is not always on point. You can tactfully deflect the unhelpful remarks while incorporating what is useful and actionable. But beware of personal defensiveness.

A customer can be rude, but you can't let the core of the critical feedback put you in a position where you can't express the value of your solutions and of the customer's investment in them. If a customer has been sharp or negative in giving feedback and you can see that the exchange is heading toward an unproductive exchange, adopt a tried and true approach to conflict management: sleep on it. Wait twenty-four hours. Or forty-eight. Or, even, seventy-two. And then, return with positive energy and a sincere commitment to incorporating the useful and productive aspects of your customer's critical feedback. Identify the factors that are important to the customer (listening skills on high volume here), and repeat those back to him or her.

You have to develop a "thick skin" without becoming tough to the core. You have to learn to recognize defensiveness in yourself, but also to remove yourself from the challenge and focus on the solution.

There is an aspect of successful professional consultative selling that relies heavily on psychology and knowledge of and sensitivity to human nature.

Finally, believe in yourself, especially as you are fed by genuine interest in doing your best for your customers.

It only works when you're ready.

Are you ready?

Debbie Holzkamp

The art and science of successful selling for business-to-business sales professionals

Part III. Engaging the Customer for the Long Term

Chapter Four
Embracing Challenges

Beyond the Business Cycle of Adversity

We commonly think about challenges as things to be "met" or "accepted," as if they are something unavoidable that we must endure and overcome. It is true that sometimes our efforts seem to be thwarted by forces outside our control, and a great deal of intense labor might seem to go up in smoke before our eyes. We know that our proposals are crafted with the best possible scenario for the customer in mind, and so, when they are rejected, perhaps by a stakeholder higher up the ladder whom we've never met, we can find ourselves frustrated. On the other hand, we might wish to identify or choose only those customers whose financial positions or industry prospects seem to make them likely candidates for a wide and active sales campaign.

Yes, of course, we overcome challenges. Yes, of course, we seek out customers who are able to undertake sales campaigns and advertising programs that yield lucrative contracts and that indicate clear sailing ahead. But, in our current and future economic realities, these customers will be increasingly tough to locate, and the competition for their business will be increasingly stiff. Therefore, for every prospect and with every proposal, we should also be thinking in terms of built-in external challenges. We should always work under the basic assumption that, even if we enjoy initial successes adversity will arise, whether from without or within an organization. It is essential to prepare for this inevitability.

In this regard, I am inspired by the words of one of my best lifelong coaches, my father, Bob Holzkamp, who has expressed an excellent example of what this attitude entails.

"We want to instill in ourselves and our customers an entirely different attitude about adversity that will ultimately guarantee success," he said. " We do not merely accept challenges, we *embrace* them, we seek them out, we greet them as tremendous opportunities to grow and expand. Without challenge, we grow stale, we coast, get fat and complacent. We need to be hungry, always, never satisfied with the last achievement, the last sale."

His wisdom comes from deep experience. During his long career as a newspaper publishing advertising executive, my father was called upon to embrace one of the most difficult situations anyone in the business could encounter when a combination of forces converged in the early 1990s to present much more than a business cycle challenge.

As I mentioned earlier in the discussion of perseverance in chapter two, Bob Holzkamp helped transition the financially struggling *New York Daily News* during a massive and contentious restructuring of that paper in the early 1990s, involving its sale to the British financier and publisher, Robert Maxwell. For three months, he worked in New York City with focus and determination amidst a strike that was called by some of the paper's unions to protest the financial reorganization. He focused on building relationships with retailers throughout the city and on improving communications between the management and labor negotiators. While the outcome is now historical record—the paper survived, to be bought eventually by entrepreneur Mort Zuckerman in 1993, following the revelation of Mr. Maxwell's shaky empire and his sudden death at sea amidst continued notoriety. The fact remains that, amidst these sensational conditions and multiple factors so far outside his control that they boggle the imagination, Bob Holzkamp *still* had to conduct business.

His practical approach to embracing and overcoming these challenges was two-fold and straightforward, but no less inspired for its practicality: first, he changed the physical environment of the staff's offices to create a comfortable environment in which staff members were able to perform at their best. Second, realizing that these physical changes would also lead to real change in the *intellectual* environment, he helped his team see new possibilities for solving any problems that stood in their way, based on open and uncluttered communications.

For example, my father had been told that there was no way to change the historically union-bound culture of the *Daily News*, but he decided that this institutional attitude was not acceptable. Rejecting this imposed limitation, he began to place advertising people in the newsrooms who could find ways to communicate effectively with the staff. Over time, they succeeded in persuading all of the employees to support the goals that both management and the advertising department were trying to achieve. "I got through to them," he said, "because we cleaned up the obstacles that kept us from communicating."

His tenacity at this time stands as an inspiring example of the core qualities of the ideal sales professional. At this important moment in the history of the newspaper industry in America, which paralleled the onset of the move from print to digital media, and the consequent economic sea change in the business, my father met the extraordinary challenges presented to him with courage and perseverance, while sticking to the fundamental values of communicating directly and honestly with people to see the job through. He credits his "true believer" convictions, regarding the proper role of management, as the reason for this success—and all of his career successes, in fact. He believes that skillful management requires not only an excellent sales technique, but also, the continual development of potential managers who will carry on the work in excellent fashion whenever the need arises, whatever the circumstances—internal or external—demand.

My father is quick to stress that he is not, in any way, categorically anti-union. He says that, as a member of the sales management team at the *Chicago Tribune*, he worked very well with its union representatives and has had similar, positive experiences elsewhere. It was an exceptionally difficult circumstance with the *Daily News*, and they overcame it by persistence and by listening to needs of the people involved.

"If you always stay focused on developing people's skills and listening to what they need from you," he says, "and if you always nurture a culture of bringing them along, your sales cannot help but succeed."

He remembers "easy days" in the late 1980s and 1990s, when they sold "pages of ads," and launched the immensely successful job-finding website that would eventually become CareerBuilder.com. Their division generated significant revenues for the *Tribune* then, accounting for thirty-five percent of the company's revenue, and eighty percent of its profit. "But those days are over," he reflects. "They just don't exist anymore." Although the media may continually change, bringing constant challenges to finding new ways of achieving our goals, the fundamental principles by which Bob Holzkamp succeeded still apply, and they both echo and extend the core principles on which I've based Virtanza.

According to my father, one principle hasn't changed: do your homework. Know to whom you're talking and what his or her cultural and generational assumptions are. Ways of communicating might change, but you can always find a way to adapt to another's perspective—and others need to adapt to yours as well. "It's a two-way street," he says, "and you need to provide the means for your customer to be able to understand you, also. Acting the part is part of the act." By this he means that you must be a person to whom your customer can relate, while still holding the customer's needs as first and foremost in your concerns. "You have to be aware of that person's approach to get to that person's level. A good sales professional will do the research to understand the full generational context and values that a customer is bringing to the conversation, especially in these times of such great overlap between generational skills and practices."

Indeed, among the greatest challenges today, apart from the generally unfavorable economic climate, are the rapid changes in technology, as I have already discussed. Younger people, especially, are bringing skills, new vocabulary, and techniques to the table that require constant change and active, ongoing development and modification of established business practices. In other words, constant change is now an inherent part of the expected business cycle.

My father continued, "But another factor remains constant as well: We are all still dealing with people. Nothing, finally, can replace the necessity of working face-to-face with customers and colleagues. When people speak to you directly, you understand more, and better. When we look at each other, we read all the cues, and we know better how to act, how to respond. Perhaps most importantly, we will always recognize—and respect— people of intelligence who know what they're talking about, regardless of their generation, values, appearance or technical skills."

Adhering to these truths will always create the right context for successful business-to-business sales, and will always be the foundation on which you will ultimately rely. The technology or the digital tools you might have used for your research and preparation do not make the sale, although they may enhance the process. Your skill at the art of communicating with people will make the sale. Finally, says the veteran Mr. Holzkamp, "You've got to enjoy it! A good sales professional sets notches. You're thriving on the challenges and the achievements. You can't just do the same old, same old."

Robert Holzkamp (second from left) with his daughter and colleagues, Chicago Hilton, 1999

Therefore, the environment of constant change in which we now operate should be embraced as a welcome opportunity and not as an obstacle. We can stay on top of emerging technologies in order to serve our customers' needs and provide them with every tool and advantage in meeting their goals. We can stay informed of financial climates up to the moment and offer our customers well-crafted solutions that will keep them competitive in this constantly changing market. We can commit to focusing on our customers' interests, and—like champion athletes who constantly and passionately train for the next challenge—work to be our best on behalf of our customers.

Turning No into Yes

We have all experienced the sting of hearing the response to our proposals that we don't want to hear. While it is inevitable that not all of our efforts will result in the sale that we want to make, when we want to make it, it is important to apply the same principles discussed above to this "professional hazard." We must embrace these obstacles and seek solutions as a personal challenge and achievement. Consider the ways to best help the customer *now*—one of which might well be to know when it's not the right timing.

An enormously valuable skill in a successful business-to-business sales program rests in understanding that, sometimes, the timing is simply not right, neither for you nor for the potential customer. If this should clearly become the case, after you have fulfilled all of the steps in the Virtanza process and considered the views of all the stakeholders, you should graciously part ways. Keep in touch through research on their business cycles or changes, with the idea of returning at another time.

If timing is not the issue, but rather, a reluctance or obstacle that stems from another source is the problem, then you can embark again on the full Virtanza process, in streamlined fashion or top to bottom, depending on the customer's willingness and extent of commitment. No matter which approach you use to reposition the solutions you want to offer, below are some guidelines that will help to lead you to the answer you seek.

- Listen again, even more deeply, to what they are afraid of, the thing they do not want to acknowledge to anyone else, and hardly even to themselves, that has led them to this "no." That thing is the key to knowing how to change the emphasis of the sale away from the thing they cannot do, cannot live with or cannot make happen, to the thing they can accept, can get behind, and can make happen.

- Recap your customer's goals and restate the objectives they share with you. Which of those goals and objectives are most important and urgent now? Is there anything else that is urgent for solving that you have not discussed? What is least important and can wait? What part of your solution does your customer like, and does it help to solve what is most important and urgent now? What part of the solution does your customer find less appealing? Can you brainstorm an alternate element with your customer? Can you suggest a second meeting to work on brainstorming an alternate solution or create one on your own and return with your best solution?

- Revisit with your customer his or her sales goals and objectives. Have him or her recap what is most important now. The alternate solution can be focused on a particular sales goal or objective out of the many that have been listed. What can you modify so that your solution focuses on helping your customer achieve that goal? Many times we have presented a solution that fits all the original needs, but later we might find out that the customer really wants to focus on one area and use only a part of the investment to achieve a specific goal. Provide that solution and you will be on your way to helping the customer now.

Maintaining Lasting Relationships

In a very real sense, the Virtanza method is essentially founded on one goal—that of providing business-to-business sales professionals with the tools for maintaining lasting, long-term relationships with their customers. If we keep the end in sight, we can build those relationships with every step. As my valued customer and colleague, Chuck Dix of Dix Communications, has expressed it, "Starting with our end goals in mind sharpens our thinking from the outset and keeps our efforts focused throughout the training process."

We must also remember that the customer can empower us to achieve a higher level of expectation, and that we must always push ourselves to gather the feedback from them that will allow us to not only provide our best, but to exceed their expectations, thus cementing the long-term relationship. Therefore, as we develop our plans for long-term relationship maintenance, the following two specific components are vital:

- Regularly review the benchmarks and follow-up markers you established with the customer in step three.
- Set up ongoing meetings to review the ROI and to add modifications that expand on the currently implemented solutions, whether those solutions are going well or are in need of improvement.

And, remember, there is always the option that you might choose to repeat the entire process, start to finish, as part of the ongoing maintenance.

Failing to follow up in this conscientious, focused manner will result in the failure of the relationship earlier and faster. But, by fully embracing and practicing the distinctive features of the Virtanza methodology below, you will find that your skills in bringing your best to your business-to-business sales customers are constantly enhanced in exceptional, productive, and *successful* ways.

- Prepare the Self, in Mind, Body and Spirit
- Cultivate the Art of Listening,
- Seek Critical Feedback and the Challenges of Obstacles
- Build Long-Term Relationships from the Outset

As we work toward achieving the customer's goals and practice Virtanza's principles in their entirety, we begin to realize that our job is never done, and the opportunities for improvement and innovation and excellence are ongoing and ever welcome.

Forward to a bright future with new rules of the road!

Sources

Holzkamp, Margie E. Wilson. Telephone interview with coauthors. July 19, 2012. Biographical information about Robert "Pal" Wilson and other family history.

Holzkamp, Robert. Telephone interviews with coauthors. June 23–July 16, 2012. Biographical information about the Holzkamp family history and the sale of the *New York Daily News*.

"Racket Probers Will Check 'Chicago Fire'." *Sarasota Herald-Tribune*. 13 July 1958. This front-page story about the arson of Allgauer's Restaurant was reported in daily newspapers throughout the United States.

Links to HDS Premier Consulting/Virtanza

HDS Premier Consulting/Virtanza Online
Web Site: http://www.hdspremierconsulting.com

LinkedIn:
http://www.linkedin.com/company/hds-premier consulting

Facebook:
HDSPremierConsulting.com

Twitter:
https://twitter.com/hdssalesconsult

Email:
Debbie Holzkamp@HDSSalesConsult

About the Authors

Photo by Charles Taylor 2012

Debbie Holzkamp is the founder and president of HDS Premier Consulting/Virtanza, an Orange County-based boutique business management consulting company, focused on companies who have a need for greater growth through business growth strategy, market share development, sales tools, multimedia revenue and optimization programs, business seminars, and sales training and certification programs. Holzkamp has proven skill in strategic and tactical planning and facilitation and has launched many successful startup products and services. She has developed sales training programs for more than fifty different media brand groups and has branched out into other industries. She is developing additional tools and publications for use by sales professionals, including a sequence of instructional books on high-level investment, business-to-business sales and strategic management, and courses for business programs in business-to-business sales at colleges and universities.

Photo by Nick Harris 2012

Rhonda Shary is a writer and educator based in the Hudson Valley, New York. She has worked at and consulted for businesses and financial groups including HDS Premier Consulting/Virtanza and the former Sanford C. Bernstein & Co. (now AllianceBernstein), and in higher education, the arts, and environmental advocacy organizations, including Columbia University, The Brooklyn Museum, Dan Wagoner and Dancers, and NRDC. Since 2007, she has also been an adjunct professor of English at the State University of New York at New Paltz and, prior to that time, at colleges in New York City and Columbus, Ohio. Her poetry, fiction, and essays are published in various literary and scholarly journals.